Living a Debt-Free Life:

Strategies for Improving Your Finances

BY

Francis T. Henderson

INTRODUCTION

Daniel got interested after hearing about Living a Debt-Free Life on the radio. He looked at the book's reviews online, which were largely favorable. He made the decision to buy the book and was astonished by how soon it came in the mail. Daniel absorbed the book, and the advice on how to improve his money had a profound impact on him. He was able to settle his bills and get a handle on his money. Daniel soon found himself debt-free and rarely concerned about money anymore. He was so happy that he had chosen to purchase the book, and he frequently suggested it to friends and relatives. Daniel was aware that if it weren't for the book, he would still be struggling with overwhelming debt. Daniel made the decision to never again let himself or anybody he loved get into debt after that. He was really grateful to have discovered Living a Debt-Free Life since it had completely transformed his life.

Are you prepared to take charge of your finances and significantly improve your life? It's possible to live debt-free and it doesn't have to be difficult. Let's look at the methods and advice you need to start debt-free living and get your finances in better shape. With the guidance of this manual, you can recover your financial independence and lay a strong foundation for your future. This is the definitive manual on getting out of debt and managing your money. Prepare to embark on your path to financial independence right away.

CHAPTER 1

Understanding Your Financial Situation

Making wise and responsible financial choices requires an understanding of your financial condition. You may gain insight into how to manage your money more effectively and achieve your financial objectives by taking the time to study and assess your present financial situation.

You may obtain an understanding of your existing financial condition and pinpoint any changes that may be required to achieve financial stability by doing an analysis of your financial situation. Count all of your sources of income, debts, and spending to start. Keep thorough records of all of your earnings and debts. Describe your resources, including investments, savings, and other assets. You may start evaluating your total financial situation once you have taken into consideration all of your financial factors.

Making educated judgments regarding budgeting, debt repayment, and saving requires having a thorough understanding of your financial situation. You can start identifying areas that want improvement or places where management might be done more efficiently. Understanding your financial condition may be greatly improved by setting realistic objectives and properly managing your finances. You may manage your money more skillfully and strengthen your financial position by taking charge of your finances by developing smart tactics and changing your behavior.

Although it may require some work, understanding your financial condition is important for enhancing your financial well-being. Reaching financial stability can be facilitated by taking the time to properly study and evaluate your existing situation. This might be the ideal time to make the required changes and go on the path to financial success.

Chapter 2

Identifying Where Your Money Goes

Let's face it: It might be challenging to understand exactly where your money goes. It might be challenging to keep track of everything, between regular bills, daily spending, and unforeseen fees. Fortunately, there is a technique to track your spending. Just a little structure and discipline will do.

Keeping a running tally of your expenditures for a month is a fantastic place to start. Ideally, you should write down your income as well as every dime you spend. Although it can seem difficult at first, once you get going, you'll notice how simple it is to keep track of your expenditures.

When examining your spending, start by concentrating on the primary categories. For the majority of people, this will comprise utilities, groceries, transportation, debt repayment, rent or mortgage payments, and associated expenses. Include any additional costs incurred for these areas. For instance, if you utilize a ride-sharing service, you might need to include an additional price.

Once you have a clear image of your primary expenditures, additional breakdown will help you find the lesser costs. This might include expenses for your health and wellbeing, such as copays and medicines, or for your pleasure, such dining out or paying for streaming services. It's critical to understand where each of these ostensibly little costs is going since they may soon mount up.

The secret to managing your finances is to make future plans. You may create and modify your budget, live within your means, and save money by keeping track of your spending over an extended period of time. You may alter your shopping list and begin to develop healthier spending habits, for instance, if you find that you're spending too much money on groceries.

Finding out where your money is spent may seem difficult, but it is definitely worth the effort. You'll be more prepared to make wise financial decisions and develop into a more confident saver if you maintain organization and pay careful attention to your finances.

Chapter 3

Making a Budget

Are you weary of feeling like you're never able to get ahead financially? Do you want to make sure you're able to make all your financial aspirations a reality? If so, it's time to build a budget!

Making a budget is one of the most crucial things you can do to get your financial condition under control. With a budget, you can discover how much money you're earning, how much you're spending each month, and how you may best use your income to make sure you're living within your means.

Creating a budget can seem like a difficult chore, but it's really not that hard. The first step is to jot down all of your income sources. This should include your salary, money from investments, any government aid or social security payments you might receive, or any other income you might make.

Then list your expenses. This should include your rent or mortgage, utilities, groceries, transportation expenditures, school loans, credit card payments, healthcare charges, and any other expenses you have each month. Once you've done this, it's time to make sure you're not spending more money than you're taking in.

Once you've identified your income and expenses, you'll need to evaluate how much money you have left after paying for all your expenses. This is what's known as your "positive cash flow" or surplus. This might help you identify what sort of savings objectives you should establish and what investments you should make in order to grow your net worth.

If you're feeling overwhelmed, there are plenty of useful financial resources available, both online and off. You might also consider working with a financial counselor to help you develop a budget that's personalized to your needs. With a little bit of time and effort, you can be on your road to reaching financial freedom!

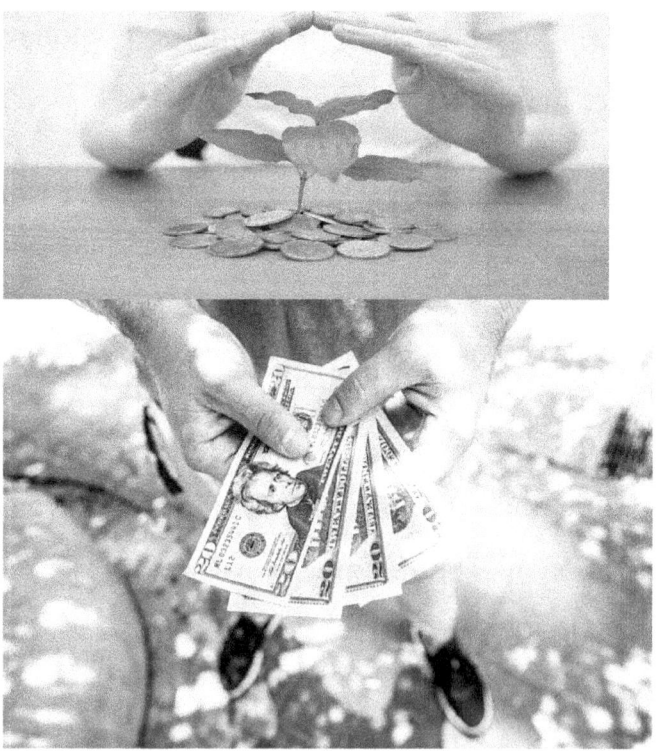

Chapter 4

Planning for the Future

Making plans for the future can be an inspiring and effective approach to gain control of your life and attain the goals that are most important to you. It can help you build a systematic approach to accomplishing your objectives and make progress towards the things you want to achieve and the life you want to live.

When it comes to planning for the future, one of the most important things to consider is setting realistic and achievable goals. Goals provide us direction and purpose, and they provide the drive that we need to take action. But before you can set great objectives, you need to clarify what it is that you actually want to achieve in your life. This entails meditation on your values, interests, and hobbies as well as exploring your potential and areas for improvement.

Once you have selected your goals, it is crucial to break them down into achievable and actionable actions. By breaking down your goals into smaller chunks, you can make actual progress towards attaining your vision while also making sure you track your progress every step of the way.

You should also strive to discover potential hurdles to your plan that could hinder you from being successful. This could be financial challenges, restricted resources, or other external factors that may lead you to search alternate solutions.

It is also crucial to keep balance in your plan. This includes carving out time for reflection, relaxation, and leisure activities. Taking time out of your normal life can enable you to stay focused and effective when it comes to reaching your goals.

Ultimately, planning for the future can offer order and balance to your life and allow you to attain your goals. It is a crucial tool for living an intentional life, and if done effectively, may lead to wonderful outcomes.

When it comes to the financial component of planning for the future, there are a few crucial aspects to consider. First and foremost, you should set a budget to make sure you're spending properly and getting the most bang for your buck. You should also consider setting up a savings account and storing up an emergency fund in case of unexpected events or sudden changes in your life.

In addition to this, you should take the time to check your finances often to make sure you're making wise money decisions. This could include having a look at your credit score and making changes to your budget as necessary. You might also try to invest and establish a portfolio of investments to help you attain your long-term goals.

Finally, you should take the time to establish a retirement plan that works for you. This could mean setting up an IRA or other retirement vehicle and taking the necessary steps to save up enough money to be comfortable in your senior years.

Overall, planning for the future should be an empowering and joyful experience. Paying attention to your finances and having a plan in place will assist secure your success and bring peace of mind. With a clear and defined roadmap in place, you can start taking action toward achieving the life of your dreams.

Chapter 5

Living Within Your Means

Living within your means is the cornerstone to financial success. The premise is simple – you compare what you earn in a given month or year versus what you spend. If your spending is more than your earnings, you are living beyond your means. Living within your means demands you to make good financial decisions that enhance your current and future financial well-being.

In order to live within your means, you need design and keep to a budget. Start by generating a list of all of your basic living expenses such as housing, food, insurance, and utilities, and add in any discretionary expenses like going out for entertainment. Then, construct a spending plan by estimating how much you can spend on each expense and setting a limit for yourself. This will help you prioritize your expenditures and ensure you don't overspend on nonessential products.

You should also construct an emergency fund and work on removing whatever debt you may have. An emergency fund will provide you with financial security in case of unexpected expenses such as medical bills or an unexpected job loss. You can begin to develop your emergency fund by saving away a particular amount of money each month. Concentrate on paying off any debt that is taking up a big percentage of your income. This will help you free up money to save for a rainy day.

Finally, shop around for good deals on all purchases. Proper research and comparative shopping can help you get the most for your money. Try to acquire just needs and utilize cash when you can. This will help you avoid unneeded debt.

Living within your means is about prioritizing your spending, saving, and investing for your future. If you make good financial choices and stick to your budget, you'll be able to improve your financial condition over time. Living within your means is the key to keeping financially comfortable and setting the foundation for long-term financial success.

Chapter 6

Strategies for Building Emergency Funds

Having an emergency fund is an essential element of financial planning for the short and long term. It's a fund that you rely on when you encounter unexpected costs or employment disruptions. An emergency fund should be kept separate from your other savings or investments, and should be readily accessible when required.

Building an emergency fund should be regarded as a priority during the financial planning process. If you have an emergency savings plan in place, you will be better able to manage any unexpected costs or obstacles that arise. Here are some strategies to develop your emergency fund:

1. **Set a Savings Goal:** Decide how much money you need to maintain the minimum quality of life you have come to expect in the event of a financial

upheaval. Be realistic, as it's crucial to have a solid emergency fund. Estimate the amount you'd need to cover at least three to six months of living wages. This will help you determine how much to save up.

2. **Build Up a Budget:** Before you initiate any savings plan, you need to track your finances and construct a budget. This will help you allocate money into reserves. A budget can also help you identify areas of your spending that you can reduce back on in order to divert more funds for savings.

3. **Start With Baby Steps:** Find out where you can save money and start with small quantities. Saving is a habit that usually builds up over time. Every little bit counts, so don't disregard small but regular contributions.

4. **Utilize Disposable Income:** Allocate any disposable income left over after paying your

expenses to an emergency fund. With any additional income you receive (such as pay rises and bonuses), remember to contribute some of this to your emergency savings as a one-off payment.

5. **Automate your Savings:** Put your emergency fund savings on autopilot as much as feasible. Automating your saving by setting up a monthly direct debit into your savings account makes it easier to meet your savings target.

6. **Make Use of All Savings Opportunities:** Take advantage of any opportunity to save money. For instance, consider transferring to a high-interest savings account or making use of matched savings programs. It can also be beneficial to search for mortgages and loans with the lowest interest rates.

Building an emergency fund may seem daunting, but it is an essential part of any financial plan. With careful thought and planning, you can develop your emergency fund and have peace of mind that you are financially prepared for whatever life throws at you.

Conclusion

Living debt free should be everyone's aim. By creating a budget, paying down your debts, utilizing helpful resources, and maintaining disciplined spending habits, living a debt free existence is achievable. With careful planning and good money management, it is possible to establish a secure financial future and enjoy the benefits of living a debt free life, such as greater peace of mind and financial freedom. Additionally, having no debt will help you acquire more autonomy in making decisions and taking risks, increase savings capacity, provide more financial security, and give you greater access to more meaningful opportunities in life. Ultimately, with determination, taking the right steps, and being mindful of your financial decisions, you can appreciate the life-changing experience of living a debt free lifestyle.